Bournemouth

IN THE *1950*S AND *'60*S

Bournemouth

IN THE 1950S AND '60S

JOHN NEEDHAM

The History Press

First published 2015

The History Press
The Mill, Brimscombe Port
Stroud, Gloucestershire, GL5 2QG
www.thehistorypress.co.uk

© John Needham, 2015

The right of John Needham to be identified as the Author
of this work has been asserted in accordance with the
Copyright, Designs and Patents Act 1988.

British Library Cataloguing in Publication Data.
A catalogue record for this book is available from the British Library.

ISBN 978 0 7509 6022 9

Typesetting and origination by The History Press
Printed and bound in Malta, by Melita Press.

CONTENTS

ACKNOWLEDGEMENTS

I would like to thank all the people who helped and provided me with information and material to make this book possible, and in particular to Trevor Humphrey for taking the time to read and correct the text. Unless otherwise credited, all images are the author's collection. Every effort has been made to find outstanding copyright owners and apologies are made to those inadvertently missed.

PART 1

INTROD

The 1950s was a time when Bournemouth was recovering from the effects of the Second World War: rationing was still in place (until 1954 when rationing of meats and cheese was finally lifted) and areas of the town were still showing signs of wartime bombing after suffering a number of aerial attacks from the German Luftwaffe.

The town piers (Bournemouth and Boscombe) had their centre sections blown up during the war, separating the theatres from the mainland, to prevent the Germans using the piers as a landing stage to disembark troops and equipment. Many piers throughout the country suffered the same treatment. Bournemouth Pier was reopened in 1946 with the head of the pier being reconstructed in 1950 and a new concrete substructure being added in 1960 to carry the new pier theatre.

The Punshon Wesleyan church, once located on Richmond Hill, had its spire topple off during the worst air raid on the town on 23 May 1943 and was later demolished. It was rebuilt in 1953 when it relocated to Exeter Road, where it stands today. In the same air raid the Metropole Hotel, located at Lansdown, was also destroyed, killing and injuring many servicemen who had been billeted in the hotel. The area remained a bombsite until the late 1950s when the Royal London House was built, today owned and run by Bournemouth University. Also extensively damaged within the same air raid, after taking a direct hit, was Beales the department store, not to be rebuilt until the 1950s and later replaced with the present seven-storey building.

The town has also experienced the results of severe weather. The continuous rain throughout the winter of 2013/14 resulted, on 21 February 2014, in 60ft of cliff face crashing down onto the promenade not far from the East Cliff Lift. In the early '50s the town saw a similar cliff fall when one of the biggest landslides for many years brought hundreds of tons of rock and debris crashing down on to the promenade below and blocking the road between the two piers. The surrounding areas also saw some of the worst flooding experienced in many years with Iford being under several feet of water when the River Stour burst its banks.

Being a seaside town, Bournemouth relied on its sandy beaches to attract its many visitors. However, even though the beaches were now fully open again and the town had reverted back to being a popular holiday destination, there were still reminders of the war, including signs warning visitors and locals to be careful of mines being washed up on the beach. Bournemouth was a garrison town during the war and for a great part of that period the beaches were out of bounds to the general public. A reminder of this came in 1955 when four children were killed handling a mine that was washed ashore in Swanage.

The Bournemouth Spartans Winter Sea Swimming Club was founded in 1951, and their members still enjoy sea swimming throughout the winter, though it's their traditional annual Christmas Day bathing that draws the most onlookers.

In 1953 many thousands of people watched the queen's coronation on television sets in Bournemouth, whilst at Meyrick Park an open-air service was attended by around 3,000 people and at the Town Hall around 1,000 watched the occasion on two large projection receivers and around twenty-three television sets. Sitting off Bournemouth Pier was HMS *Indefatigable*, and as the queen left Buckingham Palace at 10.30 the aircraft carrier fired a twenty-one-gun royal salute.

A football match on 2 March 1957 saw Bournemouth and Boscombe Athletic FC play Manchester United in the sixth round of the FA Cup, eventually losing 2–1 after a disputed penalty – unlike the match on

7 January 1984 when Bournemouth knocked Manchester United out of the FA Cup by winning 2–0.

In 1958 a BOAC Britannia aircraft on a crew training flight crashed and caught fire at Sopley Park, killing nine and injuring three of the BOAC employees on board.

The year 1959 saw the *Evening Echo* printing presses fall silent for several weeks after a dispute within the printing industry – the first time in the paper's history.

Moving forward to the 1960s, and 1962/63 saw the third coldest weather on record, with some of the deepest snowdrifts the country had ever seen, being up to 8ft deep in places after 14in of snow fell in just a few days. Many outlying villages were cut off and hundreds of gallons of water were lost from burst water pipes when the great thaw came. The snow started with just a dusting in November 1962 and then followed with blizzards in December, the thaw not coming until March 1963. During that time the River Stour froze over for three months.

The 1960s was the decade of the mods and rockers and one Whitsun in 1964 Bournemouth was to witness a riot when fighting broke out between the two rival groups on the beach next to Bournemouth Pier. These rival groups visited many other seaside towns, including Brighton. In Bournemouth around twenty people were arrested.

At the fourteenth annual Miss World contest held on 12 November 1964, Ann Sidney from Poole, Dorset, was crowned winner, while in 1966, the year in which England won the World Cup, the queen paid the town a visit to open the athletics stadium at Kings Park, only to return in 2004 to open the extension.

To get to this busy holiday destination many travelled by train, and up to 4 October 1965 there were two stations to disembark from –

Bournemouth Central, which is still there today, and Bournemouth West, which is now long gone, demolished along with the area to become part of the Wessex Way. In 1966/67 the remaining part was used for the erection of carriage sheds, inspection sheds and numerous sidings for electric stock that can still be seen today as you drive down the Wessex Way en route to the County Gate roundabout.

In 1968 the Hampshire Centre on Castle Lane was opened by the OXO couple 'Katie and Philip', and, finally, Saturday, 19 April 1969 was the last day of normal trolley bus service in Bournemouth when on the Sunday there was a procession of seventeen trolley buses, old and new.

This book reveals a few memories of 'Sunny Bournemouth' through comments written home to friends and families. It concentrates on the holiday aspects of the town – the Victorian Gardens, the beach and surrounding areas – hopefully showing just how the town and life was in the 1950s/'60s. Many parts of the town have changed, either having been demolished or altered beyond recognition. For example, the Shell House in Southbourne, a place where many children (including myself) spent time as we grew up, has now been demolished to make way for an apartment block.

I hope you enjoy these images of a time gone by and that they bring back wonderful memories of a long-lost holiday by the sea or of a time when life seemed much simpler.

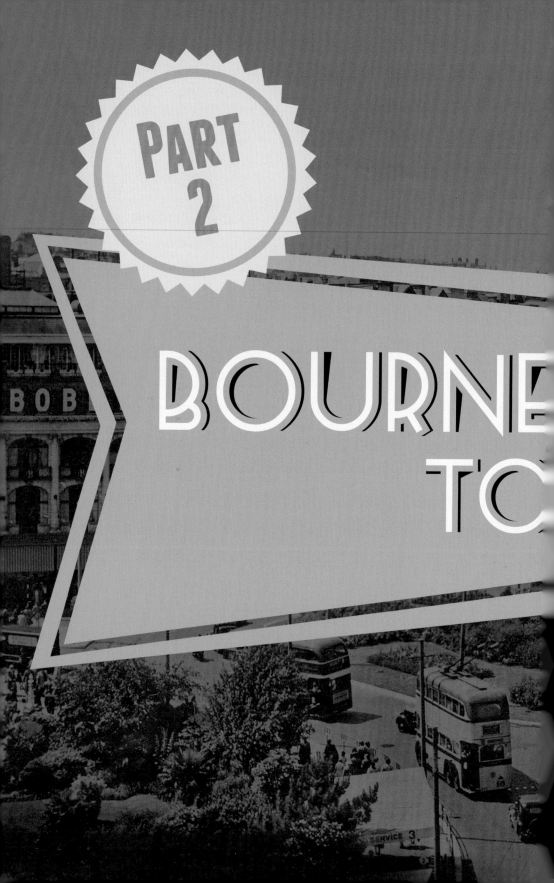

PART
2

BOURNE
TO

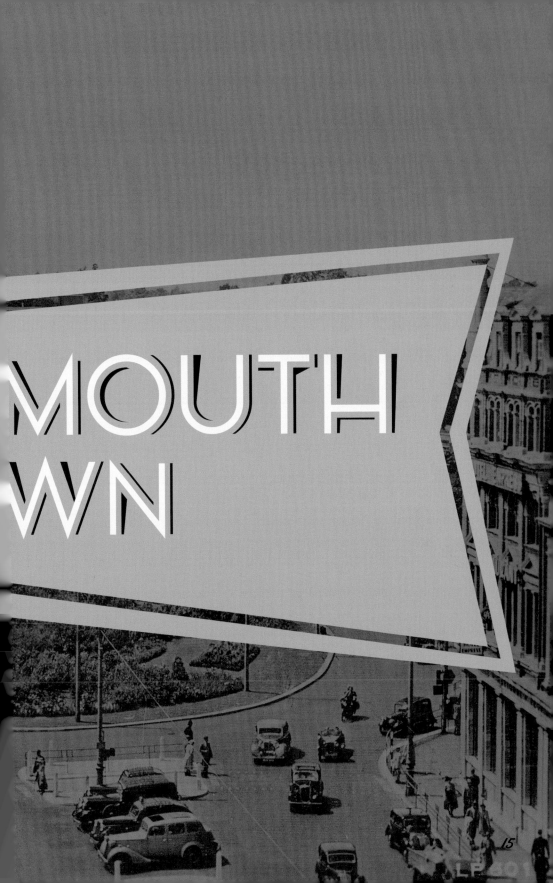

MOUTH
WN

Visit sunny Bournemouth!

A map of Bournemouth in 1964 and the visitor writes, 'It's been nice and sunny in the afternoon and evening and all looks nice' – another happy visitor to sunny Bournemouth!

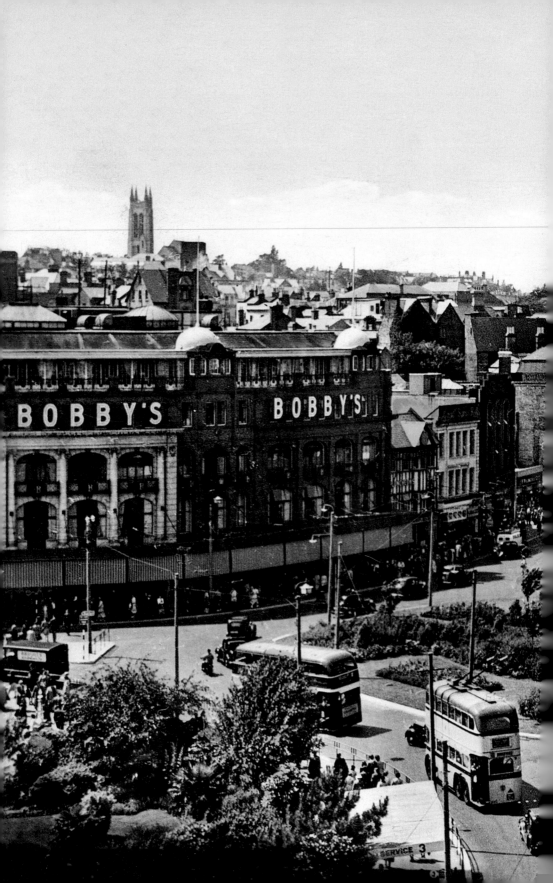

A view looking over Bournemouth Square, Central Gardens and up Commercial Road in 1954. In the background is Bobby's department store. On 23 September 1973, in a ceremony presided over by DJ Terry Wogan, Bobby's of Bournemouth became Debenhams when the parent company changed the name of their stores. Today the view is much different: the buses still converge on the area but the Square and Commercial Road are free from traffic; only the sound of footsteps and everyday chatter can be heard as the public safely cross from one side of town to the other.

A view looking down from the other side of the Square and up Old Christchurch Road in 1954, with St Peter's church spire in the background and another of the town's department stores, Plummers, to the right of the picture. Looking at this picture, I would say that it was taken from what was then Bobby's department store. Once again the sound of traffic going up Old Christchurch Road has gone as the area has now been pedestrianized.

'We are having a nice time, having good weather, the hotel is lovely and the food is splendid.'

THE GARDENS
THE SQUARE, BOU

A view over one of the best parts of the town: the old Victorian Gardens. Maybe all the people are heading down to the beach, or maybe they are off to see a show at the Pavilion. I wonder what is showing?

Another view over the Square in the late 1950s/early 1960s, with the Empress Hotel to the left of the picture. Today the Empress Hotel has gone, replaced by an HSBC bank, and no longer can you drive down Richmond Hill into the Square.

The number 31 trolley bus

en route to Winton, Ensbury Park, Columbia Road and Wallisdown on a busy summer's day in Bournemouth in the 1960s. Today the view is much different: no longer are cars allowed to turn up Commercial Road as the car in the picture is doing, only those on foot. John Collier, a fashion house, is now a Vodafone shop.

WINTON
ENSBURY PARK
COLUMBIA ROAD
WALLISDOWN 31

The PS *Embassy* of Cosens & Co. Ltd on her way back to Bournemouth Pier in August 1960. The *Embassy* was originally built as the *Duchess of Norfolk* by D. & W. Henderson of Glasgow in 1911 for the London Brighton & South Coast and London & South Western Railway joint fleet. She stayed with them until 1937 when she was purchased by Cosens, who altered the appearance of the vessel during an extensive refit. After the Second World War – in which she was requisitioned as a minesweeper – she was converted to burn oil and stayed in service running passengers firstly from Weymouth and then later from Bournemouth until she was withdrawn from service and sold to a Dutch breaker, making her final journey from Weymouth on 25 May 1967 after fifty-five years' service. Having survived two world wars, PS *Embassy* had the honour of being the last steamer to run a regular service from Bournemouth. To give the reader an idea of the cost to take a pleasure ride on the *Embassy* in 1958, a Grand Cruise through the Solent to Cowes, Isle of Wight, would have cost around 17*s* 6*d*.

Bournemouth West Station in 1964, with locos number 34057 and 80147 in the station. Loco 34057, named *Biggin Hill*, was built in March 1947 and withdrawn on 31 May 1967, being disposed of on 30 November 1967 and eventually cut up. Loco 80147 was built in November 1956 by the Brighton Works (SR/British Railways) and withdrawn on 16 June 1965, being disposed of on 31 January 1966 by Birds Morriston and eventually cut up. Bournemouth West was opened on 15 June 1874 as the terminus line from Poole and had two platforms and a 42ft turntable. The station was able to handle trains from Weymouth, Swange, Brighton, West Moors and the Waterloo lines. Services to the station stopped on 4 October 1965 with trains from the S&D route being diverted to Bournemouth Central from 2 August 1965. The station was eventually demolished to make way for the Wessex Way and in 1966/67 the remaining area was used to erect carriage sheds, which can still be seen today as you drive down the Wessex Way en route to the County Gates roundabout.

Bournemouth Central Station, 1966. Loco number 35023, a Merchant Navy Class engine, was built in 1948 and rebuilt in 1957. Withdrawn in July 1967, it was scrapped at J. Buttigieg in Newport in 1968. (© R. & M. Murdoch)

Bournemouth Central Station, 1954. Loco number 30457, *Sir Bedivere*, was built in April 1925 by the Eastleigh Works (LSWR/SR British Rail) and withdrawn on 31 May 1961, being disposed of on 31 July 1961 and eventually cut up. With the coming of the railways in 1870 came the opening of Bournemouth East Station, which was located on the east side of Holdenhurst Road. However, in 1885 a new station designed by William Jacob (Chief Engineer of the London and South Western Railway) was built on the west side of Holdenhurst Road bearing the same name, Bournemouth East. On 1 May 1899 Bournemouth East was to become Bournemouth Central and then in 1967 just 'Bournemouth'. By this time the third rail electrification had reached Bournemouth, to be extended on to Branksome and Bournemouth depots soon after.

Bournemouth Central MPD, 1967. A loco depot was built on the western end of the upside of the station. (© R. & M. Murdoch)

British Railways shed in 1961 with locos 76063, 30476 and 34053 distinguishable. Loco 34053, *Sir Keith Park*, was built at Brighton Works in 1947 and worked out of the Bournemouth depot from 1960. Withdrawn in October 1965, it was taken to Barry Scrapyard in South Wales in March 1966. Loco 30476 was built in April 1924 at Eastleigh Works (LSWR/SR British Rail) and withdrawn on 31 December 1961, being disposed of on 31 March 1962 and eventually cut up.Loco 76063 was built in July 1956 at Doncaster Works (British Railways) and withdrawn on 30 April 1967, being disposed of on 30 November 1967 and eventually cut up.

Wilts and Dorset Bristol 'K' (body no. 6766 –ECW L26/26R; chassis no. 53.89; fleet no. 199) at Bournemouth in 1953. Built by Bristol Tramways and Carriage Co. Ltd/Bristol Commercial Vehicles Ltd, over 4,000 'K' class buses were built, with Wilts and Dorset having around 121 vehicles. They were powered by either an AEC 6 cylinder, a Bristol 6 cylinder or a Gardner 5 or 6 cylinder.

Bournemouth trolley bus 223 – built in 1950 with a BUT chassis and Weymann body – on the No. 26 route to Winton, Moordown and Castle Lane. An experimental route was given the go-ahead by the council and was to run between Bournemouth Square and Westbourne (County Gates). The route was inspected at midday on 13 May 1933 when the first public trolley bus service in Bournemouth started. The service was an immediate success, the public preferring trolley buses to trams, and they ran along the streets of Bournemouth until 19 April 1969.

Bournemouth trolley bus 202 in the late '50s. Introduced on 6 June 1935 and withdrawn in July 1965, this one was converted to an open-top bus in July 1958. Registration ALJ 986, a Sunbeam MS2 with Park Royal bodywork, was in service from 1935–65. Sold to the National Trolley Bus Association in 1965, it is now homed at the East Anglia Transport Museum.

The last day of normal trolley bus service in Bournemouth came on 19 April 1969 when on the Sunday there was a procession of seventeen trolley buses, old and new. Here we see YLJ 278, a Sunbeam MF2b with Wymann H35/28D bodywork, operated by Bournemouth Corporation.

'We are enjoying all this. Had a paddle in the sea and our photo taken by the beach man. Writing this of our favourite bay.'

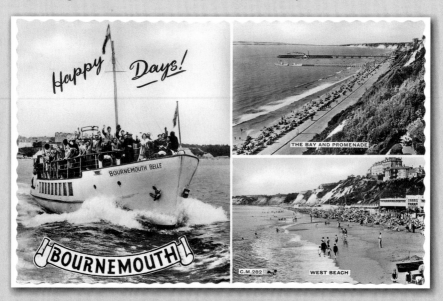

Happy days in Bournemouth in the '50s aboard the *Bournemouth Belle* (1). This card is dated 1957. A new jetty was built in 1948 located just to the left of Bournemouth Pier and from here you could board the *Bournemouth Belle* (1) for a trip around the bay or even further afield.

A day trip on the *Bournemouth Belle* (1). The *Bournemouth Belle* (1) was 75ft long, powered by a Gray Marine Diesels driving twin screws, and carried 150 passengers. Built in 1948 at the Bolson's yard, in 1967 the *Bournemouth Belle* (1) was sold to R.H. Wills of Weymouth who renamed her the *Weymouth Belle* and later she was to serve in Scotland as the *Souter's Lass* at Cromarty, John O'Groats and Fort William.

The Carlton Hotel. This card is dated 1951, not long after the end of the Second World War when rationing was still in place and the town was still recovering. The Carlton Hotel is located on the corner of Meyrick Road and East Cliff Overdrive and was one of Britain's grandest hotels, hosting such famous people as Sir Anthony Eden and Lady Eden in 1955 when they visited the town for the Conservative Party Conference. The Carlton was also the hotel where Dwight D. Eisenhower, Supreme Commander of the Allied Forces, and Britain's Field Marshal Bernard Montgomery, Ground Forces Commander-in-Chief, finalised plans for the D-Day landings whilst visiting troops based in the area.

The White Hermitage Hotel in the 1960s. As the advert for the hotel in 1963 states, the hotel is situated in the most delightful position on the seafront, facing the pier, the private entrance to the gardens and the Pavilion, and central for shopping and all amusements. The hotel also claims to have ninety-six rooms all with running water and central heating, with a lift to all floors. Does this mean that not all hotels of the time provided running water and central heating in their rooms? The hotel today is known as just the Hermitage Hotel.

Chatfield Hotel, Boscombe Spa Road. The advert in the 1957 Bournemouth guidebook says, *You may come as a stranger but leave as a friend* and tells the prospective visitor that the hotel has sea views, along with a night porter and a lift to all floors, along with a television with weekly film shows and dancing available. How much simpler life was in those days!

Meyrick Cliffs Hotel, Beacon Road, West Cliff. In 1957 the hotel states that all rooms are fitted with sprung mattresses, central heating, coal fires in the lounges and with dancing and entertainment in season within their first-class ballroom and every facility for conferences. 'The hotel is renowned for its friendly atmosphere.' Terms of the time were winter 6gns, summer from 8½ to 11 ½gns.

*'We had a very good run down on Saturday.
Weather good until this morning, but a
real soaking this morning.'*

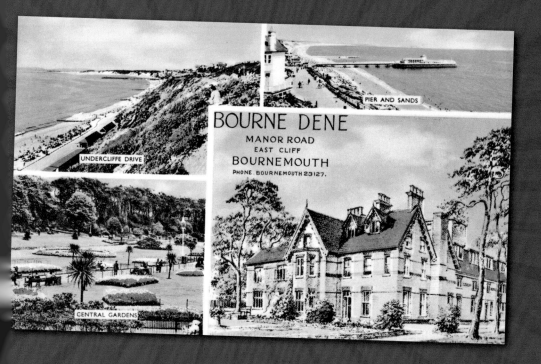

The Bourne Dene Hotel on Manor Road East Cliff is situated within a
hundred yards of the Overcliff Drive, convenient for both piers, the Pavilion
and many more amenities that the town can offer. The advert further tell
us that the summer rates are 8½–11gns with a reduced rate for the winter.
This postcard is dated October 1961 and the message suggests that the
weather was not at its best for their visit.

The Royal Bath Hotel

The Royal Bath Hotel on Bath Road opened in June 1838, the year of Queen Victoria's coronation, and was the first hotel to open in Bournemouth. In 1957 the hotel advertised terms at 45s daily and was rated by the AA as a five-star hotel. It was described as being 'set in a delightful cliff-edge garden with uninterrupted views over the bay and the tradition of gracious living is maintained throughout the year'. Over the years the Royal Bath has seen many famous faces come and go with Oscar Wilde being a regular visitor.

The Norfolk Hotel on Richmond Hill. In 1870 two large Victorian villas were converted into a hotel originally known as Stewarts Hotel, with a regular visitor being the 15th Duke of Norfolk. In tribute to the hotel's regular visitor and to the major role the duke played in English life over the years, in 1910 the hotel changed its name to the Norfolk Royal Hotel. In 1974 the building was awarded listed status and over the years the hotel has had many refits and only recently undergone a major refurbishment program. Some holidaymakers write just a few words as this visitor did: '*Pleased to say the weather is good.*'

Roysdean, No. 5 Derby Road, East Cliff. Built in 1890, this was for many years a Methodist guesthouse. The card is dated 12 September 1956 and the comments on the back say what a good stay they had apart from one drawback: the guesthouse was rather far from the sea. In 2004 Roysdean was converted into apartments.

St Michael's Road, Bournemouth in the 1950s. Today the area is classified as one of twenty-one conservation areas and as such will remain much as you see it here.

St Joseph's Convalescent Home, Nos 11–13 Branksome Wood Road, the convent and convalescent home of St Joseph and the Church of the Sacred Heart.

Plummers department store, one of the two main department stores in the town. In September 1973, Plummers closed their stores in Boscombe and Bournemouth, with many of their employees taking employment with Debenhams. The upper floors were converted into offices whilst different shops occupied the area below.

TEL. BOURNEMOUTH 49404

PEEK TRADING CO. LTD., TUCKTON
BOURNEMOUTH

CHARLES W. PEEK

PACKING DEPARTMENT

Peek Trading Co. Ltd in August 1963 with Mr Charles W. Peek in the centre of the picture. Charles was the founder of the Peek Trading Company in Tuckton in 1946 which later became Peeks of Bournemouth Ltd, eventually moving in 1998 to Reid Street, Christchurch.

Scientific Motors, which could be found along Exeter Road (where the BIC now stands) in the 1950s. In this decade the residential part of the lodge, which was located at the front of the building, was demolished to make way for the forecourt that can be seen in the photograph. This lasted for about ten years until the 1960s. (Courtesy of the Sunset Garage collection)

STOCKROOM

Y SHOWROOM

Scientific Motors in the 1960s after the garage was entirely rebuilt, with the garage offices upstairs and the garage workshop on the ground floor. The garage was demolished in the 1980s to make way for the BIC and the multistorey car park. (Courtesy of the Sunset Garage collection)

PART 3

THE VIC
GAR

A view across the town in 1962. Looking at the postcard I should say that this was taken from the Town Hall. In the distance you can just make out the *Bournemouth Belle* (1) heading towards the pier, and in the centre of the picture is the Upper Gardens with one of the ponds in its centre. George Durrant purchased 30 acres of the Bourne Stream Meadows in 1851 for the sum of £2,600. In February 1872 he sold the land to the Bournemouth Commissioners on the condition that the grounds were formed in six months and the gardens laid out in twelve months. The Upper Gardens project was completed in 1873.

Sunshine Guaranteed!

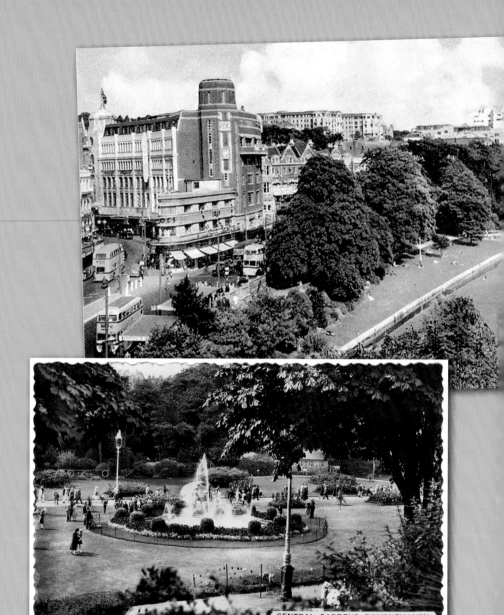

CENTRAL GARDENS, BOURNEMOUTH.

'I am having a lovely holiday here and today I have been sunbathing on the beach at Swanage so I hope I will come back to work with a nice sun tan.'

The fountain in Central Gardens in May 1954, surrounded by early visitors to the town. Today the fountain is no longer there, with the area turned over to flowerbeds and lawns.

Central Gardens in the 1960s. Originally known as Westover Gardens, in 1873 they were taken over by the town and became the Lower Gardens. During this time the area was cleared of brambles and undergrowth, with glades being formed and paths cut.

FLOWER BEDS IN BOURNEMOUTH GARDENS. 13.

'Thought you would like a little piece of Bournemouth. The weather is grand, we are both enjoying it.'

Looking across the Lower Gardens in July 1951 with the flowerbeds in full colour and visitors to the town taking in the spectacular splash of colour. The pattern of planting is still followed today and is called carpet bedding or mosaiculture.

CENTRAL GARDENS, BOURNEMOUTH.

'The first day, night gales and torrents of rain.'

Central Gardens in 1961 with the blossom on the trees indicating that it is late spring. In the background can be seen two Bournemouth Corporation buses making their way up Richmond Hill, perhaps returning the town's visitors to their hotels after a long day's shopping? If you follow the main path through the gardens you end up at the centre of town, from where you can access any part of the town. Go the other way, away from the town centre, and you will end up at the seafront by the pier, where you can take in all that lovely fresh Bournemouth sea air.

CENTRAL GARDENS, BOURNEMOUTH.

Central Gardens in September 1956, with the gardens in full bloom and the trees in leaf. Visitors to the town are sitting on the park benches with coats and hats on, trying to keep warm on a cold and windy day. In the background you can just make out the Empress Hotel, which today is the HSBC bank. To the left Bournemouth Town Hall appears between the trees, while to the right of this rises the spire of St Stephen's church.

'We are just spending a holiday here and having a wonderful time; the weather is perfect.'

Central Gardens in 1955. All the flowerbeds are in full bloom and looking at the picture I would say it is springtime, as the tulips are in bloom.

Enjoy a Scenic Walk!

An aerial view of the Lower Gardens on a busy summer's day in 1964. Like today, the Victorian Gardens attracted many visitors who could lay out in the sun and enjoy the beautiful surroundings. The postcard shows many of Bournemouth's key sites, with the Town Hall in the background and the war memorial in front, Bobby's department store to the left, the Square in the centre and the famous clock tower, no longer there today. This area is now a pedestrianized area with a cafe at its centre.

6   LOWER GARDENS, BOURNEMOUTH

The Pine Walk in June 1957. Originally known as Invalids Walk, it was renamed Pine Walk after the First World War in an effort to shake off the reputation that the town had gained as an 'invalid's paradise', being the place where the sick and infirm would come to take in the sea air and walk among the pine trees – very good for chest complaints.

'Weather quite hot, having a grand time, sands almost deserted. I enjoy the lovely shops in the afternoon, have tea on my own at Bobby's or Beales.'

CHERRY WALK, WEST CLIFF, BOURNEMOUTH.

Cherry Walk, West Cliff in the 1950s – located off West Cliff Overdrive between Durley Chine and Middle Chine.

Children's Corner in the Victorian Gardens in August 1957, with the Pavilion in the background and children sailing their model boats in the Bourne Stream. Today this pastime has been discontinued as, if you did sail your model boat in the stream, it would be carried out to sea as the grid barrier has been removed.

THE BANDSTAND AND CHILDRENS CORNER, CENTRAL GARDENS, BOURNEMOUTH.

Children's Corner in the 1960s, with the bandstand in the background and the children once more paddling in the stream as I did many times when I was younger in the '60s. Today you cannot paddle in the stream, as the notices displayed by the council inform visitors to the town.

'As you can see we arrived safely, the weather is very good.'

Bournemouth lily pond in the Lower Central Gardens in 1966, with the gardens in full bloom.

The Pavilion Tea Gardens in the 1950s.

The Pavilion from Westover Road in May 1958. Built in the 1920s on the site of the Belle Vue boarding house, it was the venue for many West End stage shows and other varied shows. Opened by HRH the Duke of Gloucester in 1929, the stage was enlarged both in height and depth in 1933 and it reopened as a theatre in 1934. There were further changes in the 1950s with the addition of two stories either side of the entrance, and then in 1968 the large fountain in the car park at the front was replaced. In 1998 the building was Grade II listed.

WESTOVER, BOURNEMOUTH.

'We are having a very nice time this week, the weather has been very good and we have got quite sun burnt.'

THE REST GARDENS, FISHERMAN'S WALK, SOUTHE

The Rest Gardens, Fisherman's Walk, Southbourne, in 1951. Originally laid out in the 1930s, it once included a sunken garden with formal bedding and lawns, all surrounded by an ornamental wall. The gardens were officially opened on Sunday, 13 June 1937.

The Bourne Stream and Pavilion Rock Gardens in the 1950s. Completed in 1930 at a cost of £13,000, this was the largest municipal rockery in the country at the time, undergoing extensive restoration in 2009.

Boscombe Gardens in the 1950s, where you could enjoy playing tennis in the summer months.

PART 4

BOURNE SEAFR

Seaside Fun!

Pier Approach from the air in the late '50s, with the Pavilion and the Pier Approach Baths clearly visible. The postcard, dated May 1958, shows a busy summer's day with the beach crowded with visitors, and the tower of St Peter's church rising above the town.

'The weather here is wonderful and the change is doing us good.'

Bournemouth in 1953. This card shows many views of the town: the Victorian Gardens, the beautiful sandy beach, and the Pavilion, where many famous people have performed in front of thousands of visitors to the town.

Bournemouth in 1955, a card that shows the seaside humour of the day.

PIER APPROACH FROM WEST CLIFF, BOUR

Bournemouth Pier Approach looking east from the West Cliff in 1954. Clearly visible is the landing platform where many pleasure boats used to take visitors for trips around the bay, and moored alongside are two pleasure cruisers – maybe one is the *Bournemouth Belle* (1)?

Bournemouth Pier Approach in the 1950s. Looking up Exeter Road towards the Royal Bath Hotel and clearly visible behind the Pier Approach Baths are three hotels which are no longer there – the Lynwood, the Rothesay and the Kildare – demolished to make way for a car park.

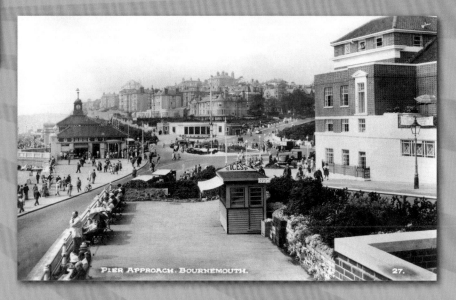

Bournemouth Pier Approach looking west again in the 1950s, with visitors on the viewing platform above the cloisters looking out across Bournemouth Beach. Today this area is now part of Harry Ramsden's restaurant and visitors to the town can enjoy a plate of fish and chips whilst taking in the fantastic view.

A view down the pier on a sunny summer's day in August 1966.
The pier, an iron-framed design 35ft wide and 858ft long, opening
out at the end to 110ft, was opened on 11 August 1880 by the
Lord Mayor of London, Sir Francis Wyatt Truscott. In 1893 the
pier was extended to 1,000ft long, only to be replaced in 1979/80
by a concrete pier at a cost of nearly £2 million.

The Pier

Looking east along Bournemouth Bay in the 1950s from Canford Cliffs, you can just make out a pleasure steamer heading towards Bournemouth Pier to either take on passengers or disembark passengers after a trip round the bay or further, maybe to Swanage.

BOURNEMOUTH BAY, FROM CANFORD CLIFFS.

'We are having a most enjoyable time so far and the weather is excellent; it is a most enjoyable tour and we have passed through some lovely country. The hotel is big and we are staying 3 nights.'

The West Cliff Zig-Zag, with Bournemouth Pier in the background and the Marriot Highcliff Hotel on the clifftop on a summer's day in 1963. Before the building of West Cliff Zig-Zag, a flight of steps called Joseph's Steps took visitors up and down the cliff face. The steps were built from the wood that was once Bournemouth Pier, a pier built in 1861 that stretched 1,000ft out to sea, when in 1876 some 100ft of the pier was destroyed in a great storm and washed up on Swange beach, only to be recovered and acquired by a Joseph Cutler who then went on to build the steps named after him.

Bournemouth in the 1950s by floodlight

BOSCOMBE TO BOURNEMOUTH PROMENADE ILLUMINATED.

Bournemouth Lower Gardens.

The fountain outside the Pavilion

FLOODLIT FLOWER BEDS, BOURNEMOUTH GARDENS.

Boscombe to Bournemouth Promenade.

View over Westover Road with the Gaumont Cinema in the background and the floodlit Pavilion fountain located in the car park of the Pavilion. I remember being taken down to the Gaumont one evening in the 1960s to see Cliff Richard in *Summer Holiday*.

FOUNTAIN AND GAUMONT CINEMA, BOURNEMOUTH.

'Going swimming today – weather is lovely.'

WEST CLIFF AND SANDS, BOURNEMOUTH

Looking west down the sands of Bournemouth Beach in 1952 at the height of the season, with a crowded beach full of locals and holidaymakers out on a hot summer's day.

THE SANDS, BOURNEMOUTH.

Another crowded summer's day in the early 1950s but this time looking east from Bournemouth Pier with the promenade crowded with holidaymakers seeking the sun. The hotels Lynwood, Rothsay and the Kildare rise up the hill towards the Royal Bath Hotel – the best hotel in town. The Cloisters, with the viewing platform above, is also crowded with visitors.

'Having a good rest with nice weather, feeling much better.'

Bournemouth's West Cliff in May 1957. You can clearly see the West Cliff Lift at the top as it takes visitors up and down the cliff. The West Cliff Lift – slightly bigger than the East Cliff Lift – opened to visitors on 1 August 1908, and would take its passengers up and down the cliff at a rate of 4.43m/s.

EAST PROMENADE FROM BOURNEMOUTH PIER.

Again looking east from Bournemouth Pier but this time in the late 1950s. Rising behind the Pavilion is the spire of St Andrew's church, today a nightclub and the spire long gone. On the skyline is the Palace Court Hotel, now a Premier Inn.

The East Cliff Zig-Zag in the late 1950s with the pier and landing stage clearly visible. Moored along the landing stage, the *Bournemouth Belle* (1) makes ready to take the town's visitors for a trip around the bay or maybe further. The Zig-Zag, which consists of a gentle incline of eight sections, was built in the winter of 1908/09 at a cost of £300 and descends 38m from the top of the cliff down to the promenade.

EAST ZIG-ZAG, BOURNEMOUTH.

Bournemouth Beach

Looking east along the sands of Bournemouth Beach in the 1960s.

THE PAVILION, BOU

The Pavilion and Rock Gardens in 1954. The Pavilion was opened in 1929 by HRH the Duke of Gloucester and the cost rose to £170,000 to develop the site of the Belle Vue boarding house. The site was not cleared until 1928 but in the meantime the foundation stone of the building was laid on 23 September 1925 by Alderman Charles Henry Cartwright.

Bournemouth Promenade looking west towards Bournemouth Pier on a busy summer's day in the late 1950s, with the tide coming in. The promenade from the pier to the East Cliff Lift was opened by J.A. Parsons, Mayor of Bournemouth on 6 November 1907 at a cost of £16,000. The remaining section from the East Cliff Lift to Boscombe Pier was opened in 1914 by the Earl of Malmesbury.

THE PROMENADE, BOURNEMOUTH.

Bournemouth
Beach

Branksome Chine looking east back towards Bournemouth Pier in the 1950s on a hot summer's day.

Branksome Dene Chine, Bournemouth in the 1950s.

'Having a good time but my goodness the wind is just too bad for words today, but no rain so far.'

Durley Chine Car Park on a hot summer's day in 1959. Follow the path down to the sea and you will come out at the Durley Inn. The name Durley is thought to have come from Durley, near Bishops Waltham, with the name appearing on a map of Bournemouth in 1805 when the land became the property of William Dean.

Durley Chine looking east, with Bournemouth Pier in the background, in 1964. The writer of this card states that the weather was not at all bad and they had a good day in Bournemouth.

THE BEACH, ALUM CHINE, BOURNEMOUTH

'My sister and I are having a very enjoyable holiday here and feel much better for the sea breeze.'

The beach at Alum Chine, Bournemouth in the 1950s. Alum Chine takes its name from a chemical used in both medicine and art, alum. The area passed over to Bournemouth Corporation when Sir George Meyrick signed the overcliff and foreshore to the Corporation on a 999-year lease in March 1903.

Bournemouth Bay looking east from Middle Chine in 1961, with Bournemouth Pier in the distance. Located between Durley Chine and Alum Chine, it has a gentle incline down to the sea. This area is a quieter part of Bournemouth Beach.

The new Pier Approach, Boscombe in June 1961. The Promenade to Boscombe was completed and opened in 1914.

'We are still having lovely weather and having a good time; we went to Poole this morning to the pottery works, have spent the afternoon on the beach.'

The Marina Sea Road, Boscombe in 1955. Follow Sea Road down and you will come out at Boscombe Pier and the beach. On the corner of Sea Road and Marina Road is the Pier Hotel and next door is what use to be the Allan Bank School which later became a hotel. Today the view is much different as the hotels were demolished in the 1990s to make way for an apartment block called The Point.

C.M.518   SEA ROAD FROM BOSCOMBE PIER

The same view but taken in the 1960s and much further down Sea Road, not far from the pier.

Pier Approach, Boscombe

oscombe Pier was opened on 29 July 1989 by the Duke of Argyll. The pier was 600ft long and 32ft wide and was built at a cost of around £3,813 with a further cost to build the Pier Approach of £938. The pier is enjoyed as much today as it was in this picture from 1969, with visitors enjoying a sightseeing trip around the town in an open-top bus.

The Overcliff, Southbourne in the 1950s. Located between Boscombe and Christchurch, this suburb of Bournemouth was previously known as Stourfield. Today the area is designated a local nature reserve and the mixture of grassland and shrubs is home to several rare species of plants and animals. One of the most famous attractions in the town was the Shell House at No. 137 Overcliff Drive, which was originally built in 1948 by George Howard in memory of his beloved son, who died at the age of 14 from meningitis. Howard raised large sums of money for charity and the new visitors' centre at Christchurch Hospital, the 'Howard Centre', is named after him.

CLIFFS AND PROMENADE, SOUTHBOURNE.

The cliff face and Southbourne Promenade on a busy summer's day in 1952 with the writer of this card telling us that *'the weather is grand'*. Southbourne also boasted its own pier, so you could take a boat trip between Bournemouth and Southbourne. Opened in 1888 at a cost of £4,000, it was 300ft long and lasted until 1909 when it was demolished after being heavily damaged in the great storms of December 1900/January 1901.

THE MODEL CHURCH, SHELL HOUSE GARDEN, SOUTHBOURNE.

The Shell House survived until February 2001 when, after much vandalism and theft from the wishing well, it closed to make way for an apartment block.

THE SHELL'S IN THIS GARDEN ARE FROM THE SEVEN SEAS

'We are spending last 2 nights of our holiday in a caravan near here. Do you remember we stayed here in 1944?'

402   FISHERMAN'S WALK, SOUT

Fisherman's Walk, Southbourne – situated between Fisherman's Avenue and Portman Crescent – in the 1960s. Fisherman's Walk Gardens was opened in 1913 by the then Mayor of Bournemouth, Dr Henry Seymour McCalmont-Hill (1911–13), with a dedication for the 'Use of the inhabitants of Bournmouth forever'. It was built alongside and named after Woodland Walk, used for many years by the local fishermen making their way from the beach to the New Bell Inn in Pokesdown. The bandstand in the background of the picture was the heart of the gardens, it hosted many bands playing throughout the year and is still used to this day.

Southbourne Beach and Promenade looking west towards Bournemouth on a summer's day in the 1950s. A section of sea wall with a promenade on it about one third of a mile long was built around the bay in 1885. This was the first section of promenade to be built within the bay. Above the promenade were built six stately homes that looked directly out to sea. The area was destined for the wealthy, but the sea was to reclaim the area for itself, washing away the beach, breaching the sea wall and crashing through the front doors. The villas were abandoned and eventually declared unsafe and demolished in 1902. Erosion by the sea in this area is still a problem today.

THE BAY, SOUTHBOURNE

CHILDREN'S POND, SOUTHBOURNE CLIFFS.

Children – with their parents looking on – enjoying the children's paddling pool at Fisherman's Walk, Southbourne on a hot summer's day in the 1950s. This was located along Overcliff Drive where the crazy golf course now stands.

THE ZIG-ZAG PATH, PORTMAN RAVINE, SOUTHBOURNE.   CM.643.

'The weather is scorching, wish you were here.'

The Zig-Zag Path, Portman Ravine on a busy summer's day in the 1950s. A rather steep incline took the town's visitors down the face of the cliff to the beach below. Not for the frail and infirm! Just up from the incline can be found the lift, which would take you from Overcliff Drive down to the beach.

Two cards of seaside humour, below and above right being a novelty multi-view card showing twelve views of the town and sending the reader a message of 'good luck', with the one above left an 'At The Seaside' card that was sent to me in 1966.

BIBLIOGRAPHY

Chalk, David, *1902–1977 Bournemouth Transport 75 Years: Souvenir Brochure* (Bournemouth Transport, 1977)

Emery, Andrew, *History of Bournemouth Seafront* (The History Press, 2008)

Legg, Rodney, *Bournemouth Then Meets Now* (Halsgrove, 2009)

Needham, John, *Bournemouth Past and Present* (The History Press, 2010)

Rawlings, Keith *Just Bournemouth* (The Dovecote Press, 2005)